Advertising

Distinguishing Between Fact and Opinion

Curriculum Consultant: JoAnne Buggey, Ph.D.
College of Education, University of Minnesota

By Neal Bernards

Greenhaven Press, Inc.
Post Office Box 289009
San Diego, CA 92198-0009

Titles in the opposing viewpoints juniors series:

Advertising	Male/Female Roles
AIDS	Nuclear Power
Alcohol	The Palestinian Conflict
Animal Rights	Patriotism
Causes of Crime	Population
Child Abuse	Poverty
Death Penalty	Prisons
Drugs and Sports	Smoking
Endangered Species	Television
The Environment	Toxic Wastes
Garbage	The U.S. Constitution
Gun Control	The War on Drugs
The Homeless	Working Mothers
Immigration	Zoos

Cover photo by: FPG International/Richard Laird

Library of Congress Cataloging-in-Publication Data

Bernards, Neal, 1963-
    Advertising : distinguishing between fact and opinion/by Neal
    Bernards.
        p. cm. — (Opposing viewpoints juniors)
    Summary: Opposing viewpoints debate the effects of advertising
and whether certain types of advertising should be banned.
Includes critical thinking activities.
    ISBN 0-89908-614-4
    1. Advertising—United States—Juvenile literature.
2. Advertising—Tobacco industry—United States—Juvenile
literature. 3. Advertising—Alcoholic beverages—United States—
Juvenile literature. 4. Advertising—War toys—United States—
Juvenile literature. 5. Critical thinking—Juvenile literature.
[1. Advertising. 2. Critical thinking.] I. Title. II. Series.
HF5829.B47   1991
659.1—dc20   91-28266

CONTENTS

The Purpose of This Book: An Introduction to Opposing Viewpoints...........................4
Skill Introduction: What Is the Difference Between Fact and Opinion? 5
Sample Viewpoint A: I think advertising is useful 6
Sample Viewpoint B: I think advertising is a waste of money 7
Analyzing the
Sample Viewpoints: Distinguishing Between Fact and Opinion 8

Chapter 1

Preface: Is Advertising Harmful to Society? 9
Viewpoint 1: Advertising harms society 10
Viewpoint 2: Advertising does not harm society 12
Critical Thinking Skill 1: Tallying the Facts and Opinions 14

Chapter 2

Preface: How Effective Is Advertising?...15
Viewpoint 3: Advertising is effective 16
Viewpoint 4: Advertising is not effective 18
Critical Thinking Skill 2: Distinguishing Between Fact and Opinion 20

Chapter 3

Preface: Should Tobacco and Alcohol Advertising Be Banned? 21
Viewpoint 5: Tobacco and alcohol advertising should be banned 22
Viewpoint 6: Tobacco and alcohol advertising should not be banned..........24
Critical Thinking Skill 3: Writing Fact and Opinion Arguments...................26

Chapter 4

Preface: Should War Toy Advertising Be Restricted? 27
Viewpoint 7: War toy advertising should be restricted 28
Viewpoint 8: War toy advertising should not be restricted 30
Critical Thinking Skill 4: Examining Fact and Opinion in Advertising 32

An Introduction to
Opposing Viewpoints

When people disagree, it is hard to figure out who is right. You may decide one person is right just because the person is your friend or relative. But this is not a very good reason to agree or disagree with someone. It is better if you try to understand why these people disagree. On what main points do they differ? Read or listen to each person's argument carefully. Separate the facts and opinions that each person presents. Finally, decide which argument best matches what you think. This process, examining an argument without emotion, is part of what critical thinking is all about.

This is not easy. Many things make it hard to understand and form opinions. People's values, ages, and experiences all influence the way they think. This is why learning to read and think critically is an invaluable skill.

Opposing Viewpoints Juniors books will help you learn and practice skills to improve your ability to read critically. By reading opposing views on an issue, you will become familiar with methods people use to attempt to convince you that their point of view is right. And you will learn to separate the authors' opinions from the facts they present.

Each Opposing Viewpoints Juniors book focuses on one critical thinking skill that will help you judge the views presented. Some of these skills are telling fact from opinion, recognizing propaganda techniques, and locating and analyzing the main idea. These skills will allow you to examine opposing viewpoints more easily. The viewpoints are placed in a running debate and are always placed with the pro view first.

What Is the Difference Between Fact and Opinion?

In this Opposing Viewpoints Juniors book you will be asked to identify and study statements of fact and statements of opinion. A fact is a statement that can be proved true. Here are some examples of factual statements: "In 1970 the United States Congress voted to ban all cigarette advertising from television," "The average American television viewer sees over one hundred commercials a day," and "Over 100,000 Americans die each year from alcohol-related deaths." It is fairly easy to prove these facts true. For instance, a historian one hundred years from now might need to prove that cigarette ads were banned from television and radio. One way she might do this is to check Congressional records in Washington, D.C. There she could find a source to verify the year the ban took effect. Other facts may not be as easy to prove. And some ideas that are stated as fact may not be. In this book you will be asked to question facts presented in the viewpoints and be given some ways in which you might go about proving them.

Statements of opinion cannot be proved. An opinion is a statement that expresses how a person feels about something or what a person thinks is true. Remember the facts we mentioned? They can be easily changed into statements of opinion. For example, "The ban on cigarette advertising has not improved Americans' health," "Today's commercials are better than ever," and "Alcohol ads are responsible for the nation's high alcoholism rate," are all statements of opinion. They express what one person believes to be true. Opinions are not better than facts. They are

different. Opinions are based on many things, including religious, social, moral, and family values. Opinions can also be based on medical and scientific facts. For instance, many scientists have made intelligent guesses about other planets based on what they know is true about Earth. The only way these scientists would know their opinions were right is if they were able to visit other planets and test their guesses. Until their guesses are proved, then, they remain opinions. Some people have opinions that we do not like, or with which we disagree. That does not always make their opinions wrong—or right. There is room in our world for many different opinions.

When you read differing views on any issue, it is very important to know when people are using facts and when they are using opinions in an argument. When writers use facts, their arguments are often more believable and easier to prove. The more facts the author has, the more the reader can tell that the writer's opinion is based on something other than personal feelings.

Viewpoints of authors that base their arguments mostly on their own opinions, then, are impossible to prove factually true. This does not mean that these types of arguments are not as meaningful. It means that you, as the reader, must decide whether you agree or disagree based on personal reasons, not factual ones.

We asked two students to give their opinions about advertising. Examine the following viewpoints. Look for facts and opinions in their arguments.

I think advertising is useful.

Many people don't like advertising because it interrupts their favorite television shows and fills the pages of their magazines and newspapers. What people don't remember is how useful advertising can be.

For one thing, advertising pays for television and radio programs and brings down the cost of magazines and newspapers. Without advertising, our entertainment would be much more expensive. Look at how much it costs to have cable television, especially the movie channels. Regular television would cost that much, too, without advertising.

Another good thing about advertising is that it tells us about good products. Commercials and newspaper ads tell us about new products and upcoming sales. By listening to commercials and reading ads we can find the best bargains. How would people learn about these things without advertising?

Advertising is the best system for helping businesses sell their products and helping people know where to shop.

I think advertising is a waste of money.

Advertising is a waste of time and money. Television shows are constantly stopped to make time for annoying commercials. And just as bad are magazines that are mostly advertisements. I want to read a magazine, not look at the ads.

Companies take out ads to help sell their products. But I don't think advertising works any more. People get so tired of hearing and reading ads that they just ignore them. And if no one pays attention, what good are they? People have become so overwhelmed by advertising that they tune it out. I think companies would do better by sending out catalogs and forgetting about advertising.

Advertising doesn't do businesses any good and it does not help people like me. If I want to buy something, I find the best products for the cheapest prices. I don't need advertising to tell me what to buy. Advertising is not useful.

ANALYZING THE SAMPLE VIEWPOINTS

Marie and Patrick have very different opinions about advertising. Both use facts and opinions in their arguments.

Marie:

FACTS

Many people do not like advertising.

Advertising pays for radio and television broadcasts.

OPINIONS

Advertising is helpful.

Advertising is the best system for selling products.

Patrick:

FACTS

Some magazines are mostly advertising.

Companies take out ads to sell products.

OPINIONS

Advertising is a waste of time and money.

People ignore ads.

In this sample, Marie and Patrick express very different opinions about advertising. Both use statements of fact and opinion to support their views and both believe they are right. What conclusions do you come to from this sample? Whom do you agree with? Why?

As you continue to read the viewpoints in this book, keep track of the fact and opinion arguments used by the authors to support their views. Note the differences between the statements of fact and the statements of opinion.

CHAPTER 1

PREFACE: Is Advertising Harmful to Society?

Advertising plays a major role in supporting America's entertainment industry. Some 60 to 80 percent of newspaper space and about 22 percent of television time is given over to advertising. An average viewer who watches four hours of television a day will see between seventy-five and one hundred commercials. What effect does this advertising have on society?

Writers like Graemme J. Marshall, a reporter for a religious magazine called *The Plain Truth*, say that advertising has a bad influence on society. He and many others believe advertising teaches people that they must be consumers. Marshall argues that advertising convinces people to buy things they do not need. It attacks their feelings of self-worth by telling them they are attractive only if they use certain products.

On the other hand, writers like Alastair Tempest of the magazine *Media Now* write that advertising can do many good things. Public service announcements, Tempest argues, promote good values and healthy living. They convince people to get off drugs, to stop drinking, or to control their eating. In addition, advertising provides necessary information for millions of people. Tempest writes that through advertising, farmers learn of new agricultural products, shoppers learn of sales, and holiday takers learn of travel bargains.

As you read the following viewpoints, look for the statements of fact and opinion each author uses.

Editor's Note: The author of the following viewpoint states that advertising harms society. He believes advertisers present the public with an unrealistic idea of happiness. As you read, pay attention to the information and the fact and opinion questions in the margins.

The author's first sentence is an opinion. It cannot easily be proven.

The author uses facts in these sentences. They could be checked by finding out Eric Clark's sources of information.

Is it a fact that advertisers use beautiful models?

Does the author think people who buy many things are happy? Is this a fact or an opinion? Why?

Advertising causes people to become greedy and unhappy. Advertising does this through the use of exciting music, dramatic lighting, and gorgeous actors. Ads encourage people to buy fashionable jeans, drink trendy beers, and clean their clothes with "new and improved" detergents. If they do not, the ads suggest, their lives are not good enough.

Advertising tells consumers that happiness comes through buying things. This is proven by the growing number of products stores carry. According to reporter Eric Clark, the average American supermarket in the mid-1970s offered its customers nine thousand items. By 1985 that number had risen to twenty-two thousand. Companies push their growing lines of products by advertising that they will improve people's lives. They convince people that they will be happy if they buy more things.

It is sad that advertising takes the focus away from the true source of happiness. Instead of looking to human friendship and love for fulfillment, people search for it in consumer goods. Advertisers encourage this search by showing young, lithe, beautiful models enjoying life while using certain products. Many viewers seeing these commercials wonder why their lives are not as joyful as the actors' appear to be. Some question why their husbands or wives do not look like the models. Others question the boring routine of their lives. They become dissatisfied with their marriages or their lives because advertising has created a false image of what life should be like.

Unrealistic advertising creates a misleading idea of what it means to be happy. Advertisers tell people to buy more and more to find happiness. American teenagers are known for falling into this trap. In 1985, American young people spent $48 billion on luxury items like video games, snacks, and music. Yet millions of U.S. teens are still depressed. They have not learned that buying more and more, as advertisers want them to, will not make them happy.

Advertisers want us to believe that buying new products will make us better people. Michael Parenti argues that advertisers do not sell products, but a way of life. Parenti is a political commentator and the author of a book about the mass media—television, radio,

MAXINE

© Marian Henley. Reprinted with permission.

newspapers, and movies. He says advertisers promise that certain products will improve our lives, giving us "youthfulness, attractiveness, social grace, security, success, sex, romance, and the admiration of others." Not surprisingly, most people discover that these traits cannot be bought.

Advertising also insults the viewer. Parenti writes that "many commercials characterize people as loudmouthed imbeciles whose problems are solved when they encounter the right medication, cosmetic, cleanser, or gadget." Advertisements give people no credit for being intelligent enough to figure out that their problems do not come from dirty toilets, bad breath, or clothes that are out of style.

Advertising, then, harms society because it convinces people that they cannot be happy in their day-to-day lives without an impossible number of products. Advertising promotes bad values like greed, selfishness, and a poor sense of self-worth. It is a fact that advertising harms society.

What is Parenti's opinion about advertising?

Advertising's true impact on society

According to the author, advertisers promote an unrealistic way of life. Does the author present more facts or opinions to support his argument? How does that influence your view of the author's ideas?

Editor's Note: In the following viewpoint, the author argues that advertising does not harm society. He believes the public knows when to believe advertisers and when not to. In addition, the author states that advertising often has a positive influence. Read the viewpoint carefully and note the use of fact and opinion arguments.

Is the first sentence of this paragraph a statement of fact or opinion? How do you know?

Can Parenti's statement be proven?

Do you think the last sentence of this paragraph is based on fact or opinion? Why?

The author writes that public service announcements help people. Do you agree?

Advertising is often blamed for society's problems. Many people say it promotes selfishness, drunkenness, gluttony, and greed. Others also mistakenly believe advertising corrupts America's youth. While advertising is widespread, it does not cause these problems. In fact, advertising is often helpful.

Contrary to popular opinion, the public is not helpless when it comes to advertising. Those who talk of advertising's bad influence assume the public is naive or stupid. They are neither. Clifford G. Christians, Kim B. Rotzoll, and Mark Fackler are the authors of a book called *Media Ethics*. These professors argue that exaggeration in advertising is acceptable because "the public is not helpless, but armed with reason." The public know when advertisers are trying to fool them.

Michael Parenti is a political commentator who often speaks out against advertising. Even he admits that most consumers know that "many commercials are exaggerated, unrealistic, and even untrue." Since most people recognize that advertisements can be misleading, they do not automatically believe everything advertisers tell them. If they did, everyone's homes would be bursting with designer clothes, cleaning agents, personal hygiene products, breakfast cereals, and stacks of beer. As we know, this is not the case. Advertising does not force anyone to do anything against his or her will.

In fact, advertising more often plays a positive role than a negative one. Public service advertisements, for example, keep the public informed. Troubled teens often hear numbers for help hotlines on the radio. Compulsive gamblers and drinkers who watch television know organizations exist that can help them recover. And through public service announcements, young children get the message that dropping out of school makes finding a good job difficult. All this happens with the help of advertising. Without it, many vital messages would not be heard.

The information-giving role of advertising is especially clear during election years. Political television commercials, radio spots, and print ads keep the voting public informed. Often, voters' only

Cigarette smoking can help you look older.

If you think smoking adds years to your appearance, remember that it also takes years off your life.

AMERICAN ✝ LUNG ASSOCIATION South Central Pennsylvania
The Christmas Seal People • Phone 1-800-555-0002

Reprinted with permission of the American Lung Association.

Garage Sale!
Everything's going.
Are you coming?

When your neighbors decide to unload their white elephants
at your expense, you hear about it through advertising.
That's what advertising is all about—advertising
communicates. About where to find a bargain elephant
(but not where to put it). **Without advertising,**
you wouldn't know.

Reprinted with permission of the American
Advertising Federation.

contact with a candidate is through paid advertisements. In 1986, U.S. congressional candidates spent $97 million on television advertising. They believed advertising could help get their messages across. Democracy benefits from advertising like this. It promotes the exchange of ideas between candidates.

Advertising also benefits us personally. Many people forget that it pays for network television and radio broadcasts and covers most of the costs of newspapers and magazines.

While advertising can at times be silly and irrelevant, it can also be entertaining and helpful. Far from harming society, advertising actually helps it. After decades of experience, the public knows when to tune out negative messages and when to tune in good advertising. To claim that advertising harms society is to ignore the good it does.

Advertising's positive side

What does the author claim are some positive effects of advertising? Does this conclusion seem based on fact or opinion? Be prepared to explain your answer.

Tallying the Facts and Opinions

After reading the two viewpoints on advertising's effect on society, make a chart similar to the one started below. List the facts and opinions each author gives to make his case.

Viewpoint 1:

FACTS

Advertisers often use beautiful models to promote their products.

OPINIONS

Advertising makes people feel inadequate.

Viewpoint 2:

FACTS

Most people know that commercials often exaggerate a product's quality.

OPINIONS

The public knows how to interpret advertising.

Which article used more factual statements? Which was more convincing? Which did you personally agree with? Why? List some facts and opinions that influenced your ideas about advertising before you read these articles.

CHAPTER

PREFACE: How Effective Is Advertising?

Reporter Eric Clark, in his book *The Want Makers*, estimates that in 1988 businesses around the world spent $225 billion on advertising. Advertising executive Robert J. Coen expects that number to reach $1 trillion by the year 2000. At present, by the time most American students graduate from high school, they will have seen over 250,000 television commercials. The *New York Times* Sunday paper alone has over 350 pages of ads every week. The numbers are astounding. One question remains unanswered, however: How effective is advertising?

Business leaders, advertising agents, and media executives believe it is very effective. Their livelihood depends on the idea that advertising makes people buy things. Many point to specific campaigns that have raised a product's image and boosted its sales.

Others, however, argue that advertising does not work. Many people who study the media and its impact on people maintain that advertising is often ignored. The sheer number of advertisements, they say, reduces their effect. The public receives so much information through advertising that it stops paying attention. Some think that the billions of dollars spent on advertising are largely wasted.

The authors of the following viewpoints debate the effectiveness of advertising and use many fact and opinion statements to support their arguments.

Editor's Note: In the following viewpoint, the author argues that advertising must work because businesses spend money on it. He presents many statistics to support his opinions.

Does the author prove that advertising works, or is it his opinion? Explain your answer.

What fact does O'Toole give about advertising?

The author uses the 3M example to prove the power of advertising. Do you agree with the author's conclusion?

Close your eyes and try not to think of advertising. Try not to think of the "golden arches" and what fast-food company they represent. Try not to remember what is "finger-lickin' good." Try not to see Bill Cosby surrounded by children selling a certain brand of pudding pop. For most, these images are deeply etched in the memory. They have been repeated so many times that we cannot forget them.

Despite evidence like this, many people think advertising does not work on them. On others, they admit, it may have some influence, but not on them. They know better than to believe the exaggerated pitches and the cheery sales speeches of advertisers. But is this immunity possible? We are surrounded by advertising. Some of its messages are bound to sink in.

In his book *The Trouble with Advertising*, John O'Toole estimates that Americans see or hear sixteen hundred advertising messages a day. These messages stay in people's minds. As a journalist for the *Times* in London writes, "Advertising works—without our knowing that it is working on us."

A case in point is an English ad campaign run by 3M, the makers of Scotch Videotape. Their videotape was not selling as well as expected, so they hired the advertising agency of Wight, Collins, Rutherford, and Scott to design a campaign. The agency discovered that Scotch Videotape could re-record more than five hundred times without losing its picture quality. Unfortunately, other quality video tapes could do the same thing. To set 3M's tape apart in the public's eye, the advertising agency created a cute skeleton named Archie to serve as spokesperson for the tape. Archie was shown using the tape far in the future to prove that Scotch Videotape came with a lifetime warranty. Within two months of starting the ad campaign, the tape had become the number one seller in England. Scotch Videotape was no better or worse than other tapes in its price range, but the public was convinced that 3M had something special. This shows the power of advertising in action.

That videotape campaign cost 3M over $3 million. But that amount is small change compared to the money put up by General Motors and Ford, who spend nearly $1.4 billion a year to promote

TEN SUCCESSFUL 1987 TELEVISION COMMERCIALS AND THEIR COSTS

	TV Spending (million)	Subject
1. California Raisins	$ 5.4	Claymation
2. Bud Light	51.9	Spuds Mackenzie
3. Pepsi/Diet Pepsi	90.1	Michael Jackson
4. Miller Lite	79.8	Jocks
5. McDonald's	344.1	Mac Tonight
6. Bartles & Jaymes	33.4	Frank & Ed
7. Coca-Cola	39.9	Max Headroom
8. Isuzu	34.1	"Liar" Joe Isuzu
9. DuPont Stainmaster Carpet	22.8	Sloppy kids
10. Domino's Pizza	41.0	The pizza "Noid"

Source: David N. Martin, *Romancing the Brand*, Amacom: New York, 1989.

their cars. Pepsi and Coca-Cola spend over $860 million a year in their soft drink advertising wars, while McDonald's spends $550 million a year to sell its hamburgers. Obviously, the very successful business leaders who head these companies think advertising works. They would not spend vast sums of money on something that does not work. Ed Ney is the former chairman of the giant Young and Rubicam advertising agency. He points out, "As recently as the mid-seventies many companies used to argue, 'should we advertise or not?' Those days are over. It's proven that advertising works."

Advertising is such a proven tool that almost every successful business, politician, and nonprofit group uses it. From Lite beer, to California governor Pete Wilson, to the United Way, people know that to succeed they must reach the public. To do that, they advertise.

> How much money does McDonald's spend on advertising each year?

> Is the author's opinion based on fact? How do you know?

The influence of advertising

The author states that many people remember certain advertisements. Is this a fact that can be proven or is it an opinion? Explain your answer. How does the author attempt to prove that advertising is effective? Do you agree with his conclusion? Why or why not?

Editor's Note: The author of the following viewpoint believes that while advertising may be memorable, it is not particularly effective.
He contends that it is difficult to prove that money spent on advertising leads to greatly increased sales. Read the viewpoint carefully to determine whether the author uses more statements of fact or of opinion.

Advertising is memorable. No one can argue that. But do we know what the advertiser is selling? Admittedly, most people can identify which soft drink is "the real thing" or which cereal goes "snap, crackle, pop." But do these ads cause us to buy Coca-Cola or Rice Krispies? Many people would say no. Advertising is good at leaving impressions in the public's mind, but it is not very good at selling more products.

In fact, the effect of advertising is almost impossible to measure. A report by the Marketing Science Institute says, "In general, total sales are not considered a valid measure of advertising effectiveness." The sales of an item may rise because of a sale, because of where it is placed on a shelf, or because a specific need for it comes up. Advertising cannot take credit for any of these influences.

Whose opinion does the author use to support his view?

Quality and price are what sell a product. Advertising can be creative and entertaining, but if the product is no good, the public will not buy it. Or people may buy it once and be so disappointed that they never buy it again. Companies like the Anchor Steam

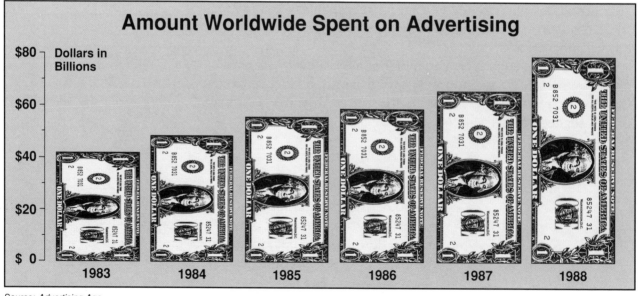

Amount Worldwide Spent on Advertising

Dollars in Billions

$80
$60
$40
$20
$ 0

1983   1984   1985   1986   1987   1988

Source: *Advertising Age.*

Brewery and Red Wing shoes do little or no advertising but succeed because they make high-quality products. People who are happy with the product tell others about it. In these cases, advertising does not sell the product; quality does.

Even Maurice Mandell, a professor of marketing at Bowling Green University, admits that advertising is not all-powerful. He writes, "Advertising is given more credit than it is due. . . . Although it might be possible to fool a consumer once, most advertisers need repeat sales to make a profit. . . . A deceived consumer will not be back a second time."

Saturation is another reason that advertising is not as effective as many believe. *Saturation* means to reach a point where something is completely full, like a sponge, so that it can absorb no more. Our society has become saturated with advertising. Americans are overwhelmed by the amount of advertising they see and hear every day. Twenty-two percent of television time is advertising. At times, radio contains up to forty minutes of commercials per hour. And the average American child sees fifty-five television commercials a day. The messages of individual advertisers get lost in this flood of information.

Advertising so overwhelms the public that they learn to disregard it. Television viewers often switch channels when a commercial break comes on. Newspaper readers look for interesting headlines and ignore the ads. And many times radio listeners put in a tape or change stations when the advertisements start. Even if a person hears or reads an ad, chances are he or she tunes it out and thinks about something else. If nothing else, America is a nation of media experts. After years of commercial bombardment, they know how to block out advertising.

Advertising is only effective if people let it work. Most Americans no longer listen to the sales pitches they come across every day. Advertisers are wasting their money. They should put their profits back into their products instead of coming up with flashier, more expensive advertisements.

Is Mandell's statement based on fact or opinion? How do you know?

List two facts the author uses to show that advertising has saturated the public.

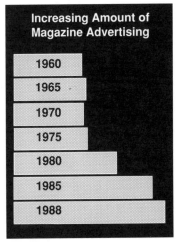

Increasing Amount of Magazine Advertising

1960
1965
1970
1975
1980
1985
1988

Source: PIB/LNA Magazine services.

The blind faith in advertising

How does the author support his argument that advertising is not effective? Can his arguments be proven through research? After reading the two viewpoints in this chapter, do you think advertising is effective? Why or why not?

This activity is designed to help you learn to distinguish between statements of fact and statements of opinion. The following sentences are adapted from the viewpoints in this chapter. Mark O for any statement you believe is an opinion. Mark F for any statement you believe is a fact.

O = opinion
F = fact

1. Advertising's effect on sales is hard to prove.

2. The average American child sees about fifty-five commercials a day.

3. Advertising does not work because people ignore it.

4. The billions of dollars spent on advertising proves that it works.

5. Many factors besides advertising can influence the sales of a product.

6. The fact that people can remember hundreds of advertisements means they work.

7. General Motors and Ford together spend $1.4 billion a year on advertising.

8. Companies would be better off spending their profits improving their products.

9. Without advertising, a company cannot succeed.

10. The average American sees or hears about sixteen hundred advertisements a day.

CHAPTER 3

PREFACE: Should Tobacco and Alcohol Advertising Be Banned?

Over 300,000 Americans die each year from tobacco-related illnesses like lung cancer and heart disease. An additional 100,000 die in alcohol-related deaths. Lost work time and health-care costs from tobacco and alcohol abuse total in the hundreds of billions of dollars.

These numbers lead many people to call for a complete ban on alcohol and tobacco advertising. Many health care professionals believe a ban would lead to lower consumption and overall better health. In 1970, the U.S. government voted to ban cigarette advertising on television. Ken Cummins, the author of an article on cigarette advertising for the *Washington Monthly* newspaper, maintains that smoking has declined since the ban. He believes that advertising bans could go even further to reduce smoking and drinking.

Not surprisingly, groups like the Tobacco Institute and the National Beer Wholesalers Association oppose such bans because they believe it would be bad for sales. They, and many others, also see it as a freedom of speech issue. The First Amendment of the United States Constitution, they say, protects all manner of speech, including advertising. They claim that banning advertisements would be censorship.

The following viewpoints debate whether a ban on cigarette and alcohol advertising should be supported. Watch for the authors' use of fact and opinion arguments.

Tobacco companies, breweries, and liquor distilleries should not be allowed to advertise their deadly products. Tiny warning labels on cigarettes, beer, and hard liquor are not enough. Only a ban on advertising these substances will lead to a lower death rate from smoking and drinking. That death rate now totals over 400,000 a year.

It is in the nation's best interest to ban tobacco and alcohol advertising. The U.S. government should promote health, not dangerous products. The National Institute on Drug Abuse identified nicotine addiction as the nation's leading form of drug dependence. Yet cigarette advertising remains legal.

Likewise, ads showing the joys of drinking remain legal even though the nation's annual cost from alcoholism, accidental deaths, and disease is $120 billion. Liquor ads inspire people to drink. Due in part to the popularity of beer ads, alcohol

Where could you find out if it is a fact that nicotine is the leading form of drug addiction? Do you think this is a good reason to ban certain advertisements?

Bill Garner for *The Washington Times.* Reprinted with permission.

consumption has risen almost 50 percent since 1960. Michael F. Jacobson, the executive director of the Center for Science in the Public Interest, writes, "Beer and wine companies spend enormous sums on broadcast ads. Liquor companies, to their credit, spend nothing. Look at sales over the last decade: Beer and wine sales increased steadily, while liquor sales are down." An end to advertising would lead to less drinking and better health.

When tobacco companies and booze producers hear the demand for advertising bans, they cry censorship. An advertising ban is not censorship. In fact, cigarettes and alcohol have enjoyed freedoms that other dangerous substances have not. Journalist Ken Cummins writes, "When pesticides are suspected to cause cancer . . . the substance is often banned outright." Banning advertisers from saying that cigarettes and beer improve one's life is not censorship; it is common sense.

It is also common sense to note that many cigarette and beer ads target teenage audiences. Though most advertisers deny it, their business hinges on getting new customers to replace the old ones who die from heart, liver, and lung disease. They need new people to use their brands. The natural audience is young people.

Michael Jacobson states, "Kids grow up in a sea of advertising. They start seeing beer and wine commercials at the age of three or four. They will see and hear thousands of commercials telling them to drink even before they reach the legal drinking age." These advertisements have an impact on young viewers.

Cigarette companies also direct their ads toward young people. Philip Morris allows the distribution of candy cigarettes that bear the trademark of its most successful cigarette, Marlboro. This example proves that young people are the intended audience of many tobacco and alcohol advertisements.

The best way to reduce this country's problems with tobacco and alcohol is to ban advertisements for these unhealthy products. Sweden has changed its alcohol and tobacco advertising laws and already drinking has decreased. America should do the same. Rid the nation of alcohol and tobacco advertising and watch the nation's health improve. It is time to stop promoting products that kill.

The author uses statistics to prove his point. Do you think they support his opinion? Why or why not?

Is Cummins's statement a fact or an opinion?

Does the author prove that cigarette makers target teens? Why or why not?

What fact does the author use in this paragraph?

Advertising tactics

The author claims that tobacco and alcohol companies target teenage audiences. Does he use fact or opinion arguments to back up this belief? Do you agree with his viewpoint? Why or why not?

Tobacco and alcohol advertising should not be banned

Editor's Note: In the following viewpoint, the author argues that banning alcohol and tobacco ads would not reduce the use of these products. He also states that such bans would violate the freedom of speech. Read the viewpoint carefully and watch for arguments based on fact and those based on opinion.

In a nation that considers itself free, the idea of banning alcohol and tobacco advertisements is ridiculous. Since neither product is illegal, alcohol and tobacco producers should have every right to advertise. This is part of that grand tradition called freedom of speech.

The truth is, an alcohol and tobacco ad ban will not accomplish what its supporters hope. It will not cause people to quit smoking and drinking. Numerous examples exist to prove this. Four European nations—Italy, Iceland, Norway, and Finland—have banned cigarette advertising. Yet according to government statistics, smoking has risen in Italy by 68 percent after a twenty-two year ban, in Iceland by 13 percent after thirteen years, in Norway by 6 percent after nine years, and in Finland by 3 percent after six years. Clearly, in these countries, advertising bans have not lowered the number of smokers.

This experience also holds true for alcohol. As Edward O. Fritts, president of the National Association of Broadcasters, states, "Common sense tells us that advertising on radio and TV doesn't create an alcoholic." According to Fritts, the Soviet Union, Sweden, Norway, and Finland do not permit broadcast alcohol advertising. Yet their rate of alcohol abuse remains much higher than America's.

Journalist Tracy Westen agrees with Fritts. Westen writes in the magazine *Media & Values*, "Ads don't cause people to smoke or recklessly consume alcohol. At most, they only cause consumers to switch brands."

The common charge that advertisers target teenagers is equally mistaken. If Budweiser and Miller are so intent on cornering the youth market, why do they advertise during sporting events? Statistics gathered by Nielsen, the leading broadcast ratings service, indicate that sports audiences include less than 3 percent of the nation's teenagers. In addition, old sports figures like Marv Throneberry and Bob Uecker who promote certain beers do not appeal to youngsters. They are well known only among sports fans in their forties and fifties. To claim that these men are trying to sell beer to teens stretches the truth.

Do the statistics on smoking support the author's opinion? Why or why not?

Can Fritts's statement be proven as fact?

Is Westen's statement a fact or an opinion? Do you agree with her conclusion?

Does the fact that beer makers use old sports figures to promote their beer prove that they do not target young people?

Reprinted by permission: Tribune Media Services.

Cigarette ads also come under attack for targeting teens. But a study done by the Children's Research Unit in London showed that parents, siblings, and friends were the greatest influence in getting young people to smoke. Less than 1 percent claimed that advertisements enticed them to try their first cigarette. In fact, the percentage of regular smokers ages seven to fifteen in Norway (where a cigarette advertising ban exists) is twice as high as the percentage in Australia, where no ban exists.

Perhaps the best legal argument against bans of alcohol and tobacco ads is it violates the freedom of speech. If protesters are truly concerned about America's health, they can take out public service announcements condemning smoking and drinking. That is their right. However, it is not their right to prevent tobacco companies and breweries from promoting their products. It is better that Americans have the right to choose which products to buy.

Name two of the reasons the author thinks alcohol and cigarette ads should not be banned. Are they facts or opinions? Why?

Free speech and advertising in America

The author argues that advertising bans will not improve America's health. Does he use more fact statements or opinion statements? How about when he argues that advertising bans violate the freedom of speech? In your opinion, which arguments are more persuasive? Why?

Writing Fact and Opinion Arguments

In this book you have been studying the difference between fact and opinion arguments. This activity will allow you to practice using them in your writing.

Four topics are listed below. Choose one of them and write two paragraphs about it. Use facts in paragraph one and opinions in paragraph two.

Afterwards, share your paragraphs with two other people. Ask them which paragraph is more effective. Why?

1. Advertising helps businesses succeed.

2. Advertising does not work.

3. Tobacco and alcohol advertising is bad.

4. Advertising provides many services to the public.

Sample paragraphs
Topic: No forms of advertising should be banned.

Paragraph 1:

FACTS

Advertising for products like cigarettes and beer should not be banned. Currently, only one-quarter of all Americans smoke. This means that 75 percent of all Americans have seen cigarette ads and have chosen not to smoke. That is called freedom of choice. The Constitution was written so we can have the freedom to choose, even if we choose things that are bad for us.

Paragraph 2:

OPINIONS

It is never right to ban advertising. Advertising is a form of speech. Banning ads for cigarettes and beer because they are bad for us limits advertisers' freedom of speech. Besides, we could never protect ourselves from everything that is bad for us. If we did, ads for candy bars and potato chips would have to be banned because they contain sugar and fat. There would be no end to the bans.

CHAPTER

PREFACE: Should War Toy Advertising Be Restricted?

War toys are any toys that glorify violence and destruction. Examples include plastic pistols, fake swords, GI Joe dolls, jet fighter models, shields, bows and arrows, and cap guns. War toys are the best selling toys in America.

Millions of parents across the country are concerned that their children spend too much time playing with these toys. The blame, they argue, lies partly with war toy advertisements. Consequently, many of them have called for restrictions on war toy advertising. If such advertisements are eliminated, the argument goes, children will lose the desire to play war games. Many parents believe it is unhealthy for their children to play games that emphasize death and dying.

Many other parents believe the problem is overstated. They see no harm in children pretending to be soldiers, gangsters, or police officers. Some point out that most people play war games as children and suffer no ill effects.

As you read the viewpoints, pay attention to the types of arguments the authors use to support their statements. There are no margin questions in these two viewpoints. You must keep track of the fact and opinion statements yourself. The focus box at the end of each viewpoint will ask you about the authors' arguments.

Editor's Note: The author of the following viewpoint maintains that war toys teach children to accept violence. He believes that by restricting war toy advertisements, the government can send a message that violence is not acceptable. Read the viewpoint closely and answer the focus box questions following it.

War toys teach children that violence is an acceptable form of entertainment. That is wrong. Adults should not give children the message that it is okay to pretend to kill people, even if it is "only fun." War and killing should not be seen as recreation. Advertisements featuring war toys should be restricted.

The number of war toys in children's hands is frightening. Most of the world's real armies are not as well-armed as America's make-believe youth army. According to statistics provided by the National Coalition on Television Violence (NCTV), the sale of war toys has increased 700 percent since 1982. And the NCTV statistics indicate that over half of the top twenty best-selling toys have themes of violence.

The problem with having so many war toys is that children become desensitized to violence. This means that they are no

© J. Margulies. Reprinted with permission.

longer shocked by violence in day-to-day life. Playing with war toys makes children think that violence is normal. Worse yet, children who accept violence may themselves become violent. Thomas Radecki, a psychiatrist who is active in NCTV, tells about a fifteen-year-old Florida boy who murdered a convenience store clerk. He and other boys repeatedly played war games together. They killed the clerk to steal money so they could set up their own military camp. Radecki, who examined the boy, reported that he was very strongly influenced by violent entertainment.

Leonard Eron is a University of Illinois researcher who has studied the impact of television violence on children. He writes, "I am sure violent toys have harmful effects on a wide variety of children. I don't think that there is any doubt that violent entertainment is having a harmful effect on our society."

Especially disturbing are the Saturday morning cartoons that look like advertisements for violent toys. Shows like "Teenage Mutant Ninja Turtles" glorify violence as a way to solve problems. The cartoons are almost indistinguishable from the commercials. Many children do not have the skills to separate the cartoons from the commercials. This makes them particularly open to the sales pitch telling them to buy toys of violence. They need to be protected from such messages.

According to Thomas Radecki, thirty-nine studies have shown that violent television programming has a harmful effect on children. Yet the government does nothing to restrict the shows. While harmful food and drugs get banned almost immediately, harmful programming is largely ignored.

By restricting war toy advertisements, America's adults can send the message to its children that violence is not okay. They can help young people understand that violence is not an acceptable form of entertainment. If children's attitudes toward violence are changed while they are young, tomorrow's citizens may learn to reject violence.

The violent influence of war toys

List three statistics the author uses to support his argument. Can these facts be checked? What conclusions does the author draw from these facts?

List two opinions the author uses. Do you think these opinions are based on facts? Why or why not?

War toy advertising should not be restricted

Editor's Note: The author of the following viewpoint contends that war toys do not have a harmful effect on children. He maintains that parents, not the government, should decide which toys children are allowed to own. As in the previous viewpoint, carefully note the fact and opinion statements and answer the questions in the focus box at the end of this viewpoint.

Children have been playing with war toys for centuries. From using small bows to shoot sticks to the latest GI Joe helicopter gunship, children have used toys to help imagine themselves at war. Doug Thomson is president of the Toy Manufacturers of America. He writes, "Most people today, particularly males, grew up playing with some sort of simulated weapon, and most of them are not violent, unhappy, or murderous." Since nothing terrible has come about because of these games, it would be unfair to restrict war toy advertising.

Thomson adds, "There is absolutely no evidence . . . that playing with soldiers has any bad influence on later behavior. Violent teenagers and adults are products of far deeper problems of our society." Blaming war toys is an easy solution to the difficult problem of violence in America. People need to look much deeper than war toys to find the root of the problem.

Auth. Copyright 1987, *Philadelphia Inquirer*. Reprinted with permission of Universal Press Syndicate. All rights reserved.

The best indicator that war toys are not dangerous is the number of parents who buy these toys for their children. Parents are very protective of their children. Remember the Alar scare with apples a few years ago. The U.S. Food and Drug Administration determined that Alar, a preservative sprayed on apples, might cause cancer. Parents across the country immediately refused to let their children eat apples or drink apple juice. If parents thought war toys hurt their children, they would not buy them.

The free market system is very good at eliminating dangerous products. Consumers will not buy dangerous products. Thomson states, "GI Joe Halloween costumes are extremely popular because young boys and their parents think they are fun for dressing up. Star Wars, Masters of the Universe, and robots sell big because children want them and parents buy them. Parents will not buy what is tasteless or dangerous for their children." Parents want what is best for their children.

The most frightening part of the call for restrictions on war toy advertising is that it takes away freedom of choice. Since America is a free country, parents should be allowed to choose how they raise their children. The movement to restrict war toy advertising smacks of prejudice. Those who would restrict advertising think other parents, especially those who are poor or undereducated, are not intelligent enough to make their own decisions. Those in favor of banning war toys want to make child-rearing decisions for the entire nation. That is wrong.

The bottom line is that parents should decide what is best for their children. Neither the government nor war toy critics have a right to dictate how families should be raised. If Susie wants a plastic gun to play cops and robbers, she should have that right. It is an American tradition.

Freedom of choice

How many statements of fact does the author use to support his argument? How many statements of opinion? Do you think war toys have a harmful effect on children? Why or why not?

Examining Fact and Opinion in Advertising

Throughout this book, you have seen cartoons, graphs, and advertisements that illustrate the ideas in the viewpoints. Advertisements can offer facts, opinions, or a combination of the two.

The advertisement below requires some thought to understand whether the advertisers are basing their ad on fact, on opinion, or both. Look at the advertisement and answer the following questions:

1. Give two facts the advertiser provides about hunters.
2. Give two words or phrases that show the person in the ad is expressing an opinion.
3. Do the facts support the opinions? Why or why not?

In your experience, do advertisers rely more on facts or on opinions to sell their products? Give two examples of television commercials that rely mainly on facts. Give two examples of television commercials that rely mainly on opinions. Which do you think are better? Explain your answer.

For further practice on your own, look at advertisements in newspapers and magazines. Note which ones are based on fact and which are based on opinion.

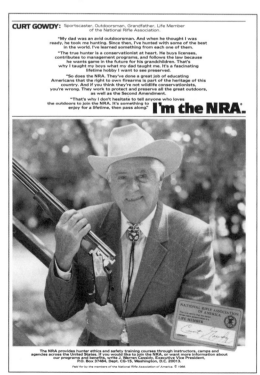

Reprinted with permission of the National Rifle Association.